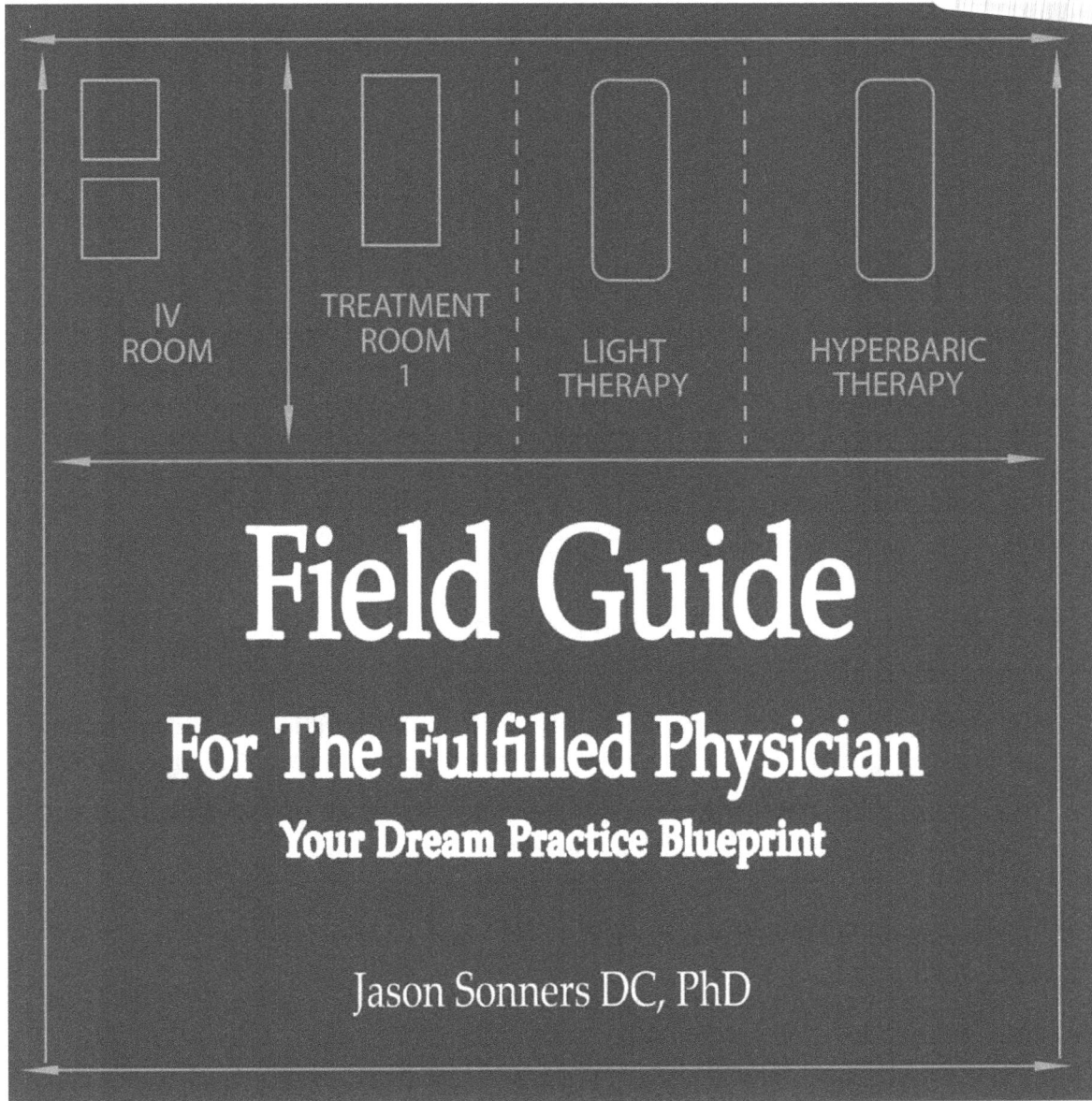

IV ROOM

TREATMENT ROOM 1

LIGHT THERAPY

HYPERBARIC THERAPY

Field Guide

For The Fulfilled Physician

Your Dream Practice Blueprint

Jason Sonners DC, PhD

publish@cbpteam.com www.CEOBookPublishing.com

Ordering Information:

Quantity sales. Special discounts are available for corporations, associations, and others who purchase in bulk. For details, contact the publisher at the address above.

Orders by U.S. trade bookstores and wholesalers. Please contact Tel: (813) 970-8470 or visit www.CEOBookPublishing.com

Printed in the United States of

America First Printing 2026

ISBN: 979-8-9915971-3-5 3 Paperback

Jason Sonners

TABLE OF CONTENTS

Jason Sonners

INTRODUCTION

The Field Guide
Your Journey to Becoming The Fulfilled Physician

Welcome to *The Field Guide for The Fulfilled Physician*, a companion to *The Fulfilled Physician* book, designed to help you build the practice of your dreams. You've already taken the crucial first step toward a more purposeful, fulfilling, and financially successful career by picking up this guide. Congratulations! This journey is about you—who you are, who you want to become, and how you can create the life and practice you deserve.

Think of this guide as your roadmap—a practical, hands-on tool that will lead you through the exercises and reflections necessary to create a practice that reflects your values, serves your ideal patients, and gives you the freedom and joy you've always wanted. This is not just a workbook; it's a transformative journey designed to help you discover the answers within yourself. It is the catalyst that will allow you to dream big, take action, and build something extraordinary.

What Is This Field Guide?

The Field Guide is the action-oriented companion to *The Fulfilled Physician*. It's meant to be interactive. Each assignment, exercise, and reflection builds on the next, guiding you through the foundational steps to becoming the physician and the leader you've always envisioned.

This guide will help you clarify your "why," visualize your ideal practice, and create the systems, habits, and mindsets necessary to make that vision a reality. These aren't abstract exercises. The insights you gain will help shape the decisions you make, from how you interact with patients and staff to how you structure your day-to-day operations.

The journey you're about to take is as personal as it is professional. The exercises in this guide challenge you to dig deep and reflect not just on what you want to do but also on who you want to be as a practitioner, leader, and person. This clarity of purpose will fuel your success.

Why Is This Important?

In a world where healthcare practitioners are often bogged down by bureaucracy, stress, and burnout, it's easy to lose sight of why you chose this path in the first place. That's where *The Fulfilled Physician* and this Field Guide come in. By aligning your mission with the purpose of your practice, you'll find new ways to thrive—not just financially but emotionally and spiritually as well.

Jason Sonners

This guide is your key to a practice that doesn't just *work*—it *works for you.* It's designed to help you cultivate a space where you can do what you love, provide exceptional care, and foster a supportive environment for yourself, your team, and your patients. It's about shifting from survival mode to a life where you thrive, lead, and grow.

What Will You Achieve?

Imagine stepping into your office every day excited and energized, surrounded by a team that shares your vision and patients who appreciate the care you provide. Imagine having the financial freedom to focus on what really matters and the emotional fulfillment that comes from running a practice that aligns with your core values. That's the vision *The Field Guide For The Fulfilled Physician* holds for you.

By following this guide, you'll:

- **Clarify Your Purpose**: Understand what drives you, how to align your practice with your values, and how to build a career that feels meaningful.

- **Create Your Ideal Vision**: Craft a vivid picture of the practice you want to create, down to the most minor details, so you know exactly where you're headed.

- **Identify Your Ideal Client**: Learn who your ideal patients are and how to attract, nurture, and serve them in a way that benefits both them and your practice.

Jason Sonners

- **Build a Purpose-Driven Practice**: Establish systems that support not only the business but also your growth, joy, and fulfillment.

A Journey to Fulfillment

This guide isn't just about creating a successful practice; it's about making the *proper* practice for *you*. It's about discovering the things that bring you joy, motivate you to show up each day, and help you leave a lasting impact on the lives of your patients and your community.

As you work through the exercises, remember that this process is about progress, not perfection. Some parts will be easy, while others may push you out of your comfort zone—but every step is designed to bring you closer to the practice and life you've always dreamed of. You deserve this.

The journey to becoming a Fulfilled Physician is one of growth, self-discovery, and ultimately, empowerment. The more you engage with this guide, the more you will unlock the tools, clarity, and mindset necessary to build the practice you've always wanted. Every page, every exercise, is a stepping stone to a future where you thrive both personally and professionally.

Let's get started! You have everything within you to create the life and practice of your dreams—and this Workbook Field Guide is here to help you make it a reality.

Here's to your future success and fulfillment.

Welcome to the journey. You're right where you need to be. Let's build the practice of your dreams together.

Jason Sonners

IT BEGINS WITH YOU

Chapter 1 of *The Fulfilled Physician*, "It Begins with You," emphasizes that the foundation of a successful healthcare practice is rooted in the practitioner's identity and values. The core message is that who you are—your personal and professional identity—shapes the quality of care you provide, the relationships you build, and the success of your business. It stresses that a precise alignment between your internal values and external actions is essential to building trust and credibility with patients and staff.

The Chapter introduces the **Be, Do, Have** model, a foundational framework for success. This model urges practitioners first to embody **the qualities** they want to represent (Be), then **take actions** that align with those qualities (Do), which will ultimately lead to achieving their goals (Have). It highlights that many people mistakenly focus on actions (Do) or desired outcomes (Have) without first becoming the person capable of achieving those goals. By focusing on "who you are," you can create the mindset and behaviors necessary for success.

Practitioners are encouraged to reflect on critical questions about their identity and vision:

- Who are you now?
- Who do you want to become?
- What is your vision for the future?

These reflections help align one's actions with long-term goals, guiding decisions related to patient care, staff management, and business strategy.

The Chapter also emphasizes the importance of **consistency** in your practice. Your daily interactions with patients and staff should reflect the same core values that define your professional mission. This builds credibility and fosters a positive culture within your practice. Additionally, clear and compassionate communication with patients is highlighted as a critical factor in demonstrating care and building strong relationships.

Another key takeaway is the importance of becoming comfortable with discomfort. Growth in any business, especially in healthcare, often involves stepping outside of one's comfort zone. Whether it's learning new business skills, adopting new technologies, or expanding services, practitioners must be willing to face challenges head-on. The Chapter encourages embracing discomfort as a path to personal and professional development.

Finally, Chapter 1 concludes by explaining that practitioners should proactively embody their mission. By living out the values that define their practice, healthcare professionals can foster stronger patient relationships, increase trust, and build a practice that not only fulfills professional aspirations but also makes a meaningful impact on the community. Through the **Be, Do, Have** model, healthcare providers can continuously grow, refine their practices, and achieve their vision of success.

This Chapter sets the stage for the rest of the book by providing a mindset and framework to guide healthcare professionals in building both a fulfilling career and a thriving practice.

- o Reflect on Your Why: Take some time to think deeply about why you want to start or transform your practice. Write down your reasons, both external and internal. What experiences in your life have shaped your desire to create the practice of your dreams? How will your "why" guide your decisions and actions as you build your practice?

1. Why is it so important for you to take this journey?

_____

_____

_____

_____

_____

_____

2. What impact will it have on the lives of the people you serve?

_____

_____

_____

_____

_____

3. What impact will it have on your life? And your loved ones?

_____

_____

_____

_____

_____

For the exercise, let's look at the professional area of your life (career) and specifically the Be you want to become or to hone who you already are simply:

- o List ten characteristics you believe the person who already has the practice of their dreams embodies. These can absolutely be characteristics you already have, but they should also include ones you have but want to improve on and ones you may not have yet. Think about your colleagues, your mentors, and other people in your field, and generate your list now. Then, give yourself an honest score, 0-10, on how much of that characteristic you currently already embody.

Jason Sonners

	Characteristic	Current Score (0-10)
1		
2		
3		
4		
5		
6		
7		
8		
9		
10		

o Next, use the Space Below and describe two particular examples of when you displayed each of these traits (if you have any examples). Under that, describe two examples of when you wished you could display this trait, but whatever series of reasons you displayed something else.

Characteristic: #1 _____

_____

_____

_____

_____

Jason Sonners

Describe a time you expressed this characteristic well:

_____

_____

_____

_____

_____

_____

_____

_____

Describe a time you wished you responded better:

_____

_____

_____

_____

_____

_____

_____

_____

_____

Describe how you could have responded or behaved more in one with this characteristic:

_____

_____

_____

Characteristic: #2 _____

_____

_____

Describe a time you expressed this characteristic well: _____

_____

_____

_____

_____

_____

_____

Describe a time you wished you responded better: _____

_____

_____

_____

_____

Describe how you could have responded or behaved more in one with this characteristic:

_____

_____

_____

Characteristic: #3 _____

_____

_____

Describe a time you expressed this characteristic well: _____

_____

_____

_____

_____

_____

_____

Describe a time you wished you responded better:
_____

_____

_____

_____

_____

_____

_____

_____

_____

_____

Describe how you could have responded or behaved more in one with this characteristic:

_____

_____

Characteristic: #4 _____

_____

_____

Describe a time you expressed this characteristic well: _____

_____

_____

_____

_____

_____

_____

_____

_____

Describe a time you wished you responded better: _____

_____

_____

_____

_____

_____

_____

Describe how you could have responded or behaved more in one with this characteristic: _____

_____

_____

Characteristic: #5 _____

_____

_____

Describe a time you expressed this characteristic well:

_____

_____

_____

_____

_____

_____

_____

_____

Describe a time you wished you responded better:

_____

_____

_____

_____

_____

_____

_____

_____

Describe how you could have responded or behaved more in one with this characteristic:

_____

_____

_____

_____

_____

_____

_____

_____

While this activity takes some time to think through and may feel monotonous or mundane, it is critically important. if you find yourself continuously in a pattern you do not like or want. So if you wish you could change your response and reaction to certain people or certain situations, you need to identify these responses, reactions and patterns ahead of time. Understand what went wrong, rewrite the script for how you wish it went and then practice your new responses and new scripts. Much like in sports, you do not show up on game day and hope that new plays or new strategies are going to be successful. you spend weeks and months practicing so that on game day, they are essentially second nature. The same is true in our business and with our relationships. This exercise is simply one way to begin making these changes.

Jason Sonners

THE POWER OF VISION

Chapter 2 of *The Fulfilled Physician*, "The Power of Vision," stresses the importance of having a clear and defined vision before building a successful healthcare practice. The Chapter is grounded in Stephen Covey's concept of "Begin with the End in Mind." This principle encourages practitioners to visualize their ultimate goals and desired outcomes, allowing them to shape every decision and action in alignment with that long-term vision.

The Chapter emphasizes that **vision acts as a guiding force**—a mental picture of what you want to create or accomplish in your practice. A well-defined vision helps keep you motivated, especially during challenging times, and ensures that your actions consistently move you toward your goals. Having this clarity allows healthcare professionals to focus on opportunities and eliminate distractions that don't contribute to their overall mission.

In addition to vision, **finding your voice** is highlighted as an essential part of the journey. Covey's concept of "finding your voice" refers to identifying your unique talents, passions, and values and using them to make a meaningful contribution to the world. For healthcare practitioners, this means aligning their professional activities with their core purpose and communicating this alignment clearly to both patients and staff. By tapping into these inner values, practitioners can inspire and empower others around them—creating a practice that thrives on collaboration, creativity, and purpose.

The Chapter also introduces the concept of **team empowerment** as a critical factor for exponential growth. Drawing inspiration from the book *10x Is Easier Than 2x*, the idea is that investing in the development and purpose of your team can unlock exponential progress in your practice. This involves helping team members identify their unique strengths and creating a supportive environment where they can grow and contribute meaningfully. When staff members feel aligned with the practice's mission and empowered in their roles, the practice becomes self-regulating and driven by a shared sense of purpose.

The practical application of these concepts involves a clear strategy for building the vision of your practice:

- **Define your ideal practice**: This includes details about the physical space, patient experience, and services offered.
- **Build a supportive team**: Identify the qualities you want in your staff and create an environment that nurtures growth and collaboration.
- **Understand your patients**: Visualize the ideal patient demographic and the relationships you want to build with them.

- **Consistency**: Ensure every aspect of your practice, from operations to patient interactions, reflects your vision.

By crafting a **vision board** and a detailed description of their dream practice, practitioners can begin to make strategic decisions that align with their goals. The Chapter concludes by encouraging healthcare professionals to refine and revisit their vision as their practice grows continuously. By staying connected to this vision, practitioners ensure that every step they take brings them closer to their ideal practice.

Describe your ideal "dream" practice: This is your place to DREAM! Write a detailed description of your ideal practice. What does it look like? How does it feel? What kind of care do you provide? Who are your patients? Be as specific and vivid as possible. Colors, visuals, sounds, smells, office flow, conversations in your reception area, how people are dressed, describe your ideal staff and your ideal patients coming through the doors.
This should be a no-rules, super detailed description of the vision for the office and business. Who works there? What do they do? What type of location is this? How visible and accessible is it for your ideal clients? Who are your ideal clients? What does the building look like, and what do the offices and reception look like? What colors are the walls; what type of lighting, pictures, marketing materials, and anything else are decorating the office?

_____

_____

_____

_____

_____

_____

_____

_____

_____

_____

_____

_____

_____

_____

_____

_____

_____

_____

_____

_____

_____

_____

_____

_____

_____

Create your vision board: Using a large sheet of paper or a digital tool, create a vision board for your practice. Include images, words, and phrases that represent the physical space, the services you'll offer, the team you'll build, and the patients you'll serve. Let your imagination run wild—this is your opportunity to dream big.

How do we treat people, and how do we answer the phone? What is the feeling people should have when they walk in? What feeling should they have on the way out? What type of employees do you have? What positions do you need to be filled?

Does your staff have a growth mindset like you? The more time you spend here, the more detail you create, the more likely you will reach your vision, and the more likely you will know when you've reached your goals.

The Be: Are the characteristics you built out in the *Field Guide* consistent here as well? Are there any other characteristics you need to add or take away from your original list for the person who would have already reached this level of practice success?

Define your ideal workday: Imagine a typical day in your future practice. From working in the morning through the entire workday, evening and going to bed, please describe your **Ideal Day**. Specifically the Flow of the office.

	MON	TUE	WED	THU	FRI	SAT	SUN
6 am							
7 am							
8 am							
9 am							
10 am							
11 am							
12 pm							
1 pm							
2 pm							
3 pm							
4 pm							
5 pm							
6 pm							
7 pm							
8 pm							
9 pm							
10 pm							
11 pm							

Jason Sonners

Characteristic additions
_____

_____

_____

_____

_____

_____

_____

_____

_____

_____

_____

_____

_____

_____

_____

_____

_____

_____

Characteristic subtractions

_____

_____

_____

_____

_____

_____

_____

_____

_____

_____

_____

_____

_____

_____

_____

_____

_____

_____

Jason Sonners

MAPPING YOUR PURPOSE

Chapter 3 of *The Fulfilled Physician*, titled "Mapping Your Purpose," focuses on defining the **purpose, mission, and vision** of a healthcare practice. It emphasizes that a well-defined purpose is the driving force behind a successful practice, shaping decision-making, guiding growth, and maintaining alignment with long-term goals. Practitioners are encouraged to reflect deeply on their purpose, which will serve as their compass, motivating them through challenges and helping them stay focused on their broader vision.

The Chapter outlines the difference between **purpose, mission, and vision**:

- **Purpose**: The core reason why you do what you do. It answers the "why" behind your practice and is essential for sustaining motivation, especially when facing difficulties. Purpose reflects the deeper meaning behind your work and how it impacts both patients and the community.

- **Mission**: A concise statement describing what your practice offers and how it sets itself apart from others. The mission acts as a clear guide for what your practice strives to accomplish on a daily basis.
- **Vision**: A long-term picture of where you want your practice to go. It's the destination you're working toward and represents the future impact your practice will have on your patients, staff, and community.

By defining these three key elements, healthcare practitioners create a solid foundation for building a thriving practice. The Chapter stresses that **purpose should be at the center of everything**. When you align your business decisions with your purpose, you ensure that every action and strategy is meaningful and contributes to long-term success.

The concept of **core values** is also explored in depth. Values serve as the compass for maintaining direction throughout the practice's journey. Defining and committing to a set of non-negotiable core values helps guide daily decisions, ensure consistency in patient care, and foster a positive and aligned workplace culture. These values should resonate with both staff and patients, ensuring everyone involved in the practice is working toward the same goals.

Chapter 3 also introduces the Japanese concept of **Ikigai**, which translates to "reason for being." Ikigai is seen as the intersection of four elements:

1. **What you love (passion)**
2. **What the world needs (mission)**
3. **What you are good at (vocation)**

4. **What you can be paid for (profession)**

By finding the balance between these elements, practitioners can align their personal and professional lives, creating a practice that brings them joy and fulfillment while also meeting the needs of their patients. Achieving Ikigai ensures that a practice is not only profitable but also purpose-driven and personally rewarding.

The Chapter encourages practitioners to frequently revisit and revise their purpose, mission, vision, and values as their practice evolves. These elements are not static but should grow and adapt as the practice matures and as new insights are gained. By doing this, practitioners can maintain alignment with their goals and continue to build a practice that reflects their deepest values and aspirations.

Finally, Chapter 3 concludes by emphasizing that understanding your purpose provides clarity and focus. When difficult decisions arise or when challenges emerge, practitioners can turn to their purpose and core values to guide them. This precise alignment between purpose, mission, vision, and values creates a unified approach that benefits patients, staff, and the broader community.

In summary, Chapter 3 highlights that **purpose is the foundation of a successful practice**. By clearly defining and aligning your purpose, mission, vision, and values, you create a roadmap for long-term success and fulfillment in both your personal and professional life.

Please refer to page 45 in Chapter 3 for more details.

The following assignments are really building and defining yourself and your practice so that people who share your vision know they aligned with you and choose to come along for the ride.....

Vision: Your Destination

Purpose: Your reason for embarking on this journey

Mission: Your map, your paradigm, how will you get to your destination?

Core Values: Your compass, the tools you use to keep yourself on track!

Clarify your Vision: Take time to write a clear and concise purpose statement for your practice. Why are you in this business? What drives you? How will this purpose influence the way you run your practice and the care you provide? This is a clear sentence that summarizes your "dream" exercise from the last Chapter.

_____

_____

_____

_____

_____

_____

_____

State your vision, in a single clear and concise sentence:
My (our) vision is......

_____

_____

_____

_____

_____

_____

State your purpose: Let people know why you are doing what you're doing!
Why is this so important?
My (our) vision is......

_____

_____

_____

_____

_____

_____

Share your Mission: Draft your mission statements. Your mission should be a brief description of what you offer and how you will achieve your vision.

Jason Sonners

My (our) vision is......

_____

_____

_____

_____

_____

_____

_____

_____

_____

Identify core values: List the core values that will guide your practice. How do these values shape your approach to patient care and team collaboration? How will you ensure every aspect of your practice reflect these values?

Remember to view the examples I shared with you from my businesses in the book's appendix if you'd like to get ideas or see a few different structures of what this might look like.

IDENTIFYING YOUR IDEAL CLIENT

Chapter 4 of *The Fulfilled Physician*, "Identifying Your Ideal Client," emphasizes the importance of defining and understanding your ideal client as a key step in building a successful healthcare practice. Attracting the right clients is essential for long-term success, as it allows practitioners to serve those who align with the practice's core values, mission, and goals.

The Chapter starts by explaining that knowing who your **ideal client** is begins with identifying your **niche market**. This involves considering demographics (age, gender, location, income level) and **psychographics** (values, lifestyle choices, and attitudes). The goal is to define a specific client profile that is best suited for your practice's services. By narrowing down who your ideal client is, you can tailor your marketing, communication, and service offerings to meet their needs more effectively.

To help define an ideal client, the Chapter suggests focusing on several key factors:

1. **Demographics**: Characteristics like age, gender, income, and location that help pinpoint your target audience. For example, are you

targeting young professionals, families, or older adults?

2. **Psychographics**: These go beyond demographics and include values, beliefs, and attitudes. Understanding what your clients care about, such as holistic health or preventive care, can help you craft services that align with their lifestyles.

3. **Health Needs**: Identify the specific health concerns or conditions that your ideal clients are likely to have. This helps you develop specialized services or treatment plans that cater directly to their needs.

4. **Communication Preferences**: Understand how your ideal clients prefer to communicate—whether through in-person meetings, phone calls, or digital platforms. This will allow you to engage with them in the way they feel most comfortable.

By defining these characteristics, practitioners can better target their marketing and tailor their patient care to attract the right clients. The Chapter also underscores the importance of aligning your ideal client with your **core values**, as building a practice with clients who share your values ensures smoother, more fulfilling relationships. Not many things are worse than going on a long journey with people with whom you don't share the same fundamental values.

The Chapter also delves into **attracting the right clients**. It encourages practitioners to create messaging that speaks directly to their ideal audience, using clear language that reflects the services they offer and the value they bring to patients' lives. By doing so, practitioners can create a practice where both the patients and the staff feel connected to a shared purpose and are more likely to remain loyal long-term.

Jason Sonners

In addition to defining and attracting the ideal client, the Chapter advises practitioners to assess their **current patient base** to identify common characteristics among their most successful client relationships. This reflection can help fine-tune who the practice should continue to serve and how to improve relationships with future clients.

Finally, the Chapter explains that continuously refining your understanding of your ideal client is essential as both market trends and client expectations evolve. By staying updated on the needs and preferences of your target audience, you ensure that your practice remains relevant and aligned with the clients who will help it grow.

Please refer to page 61 in Chapter 4 for more details.

Identify your white flag and red flag clients: Reflect on your past experiences with patients. Make a list of your white flag clients—the ones who brought you joy and success. What characteristics do they share? Now, list your red flag clients— the ones who drained your energy or disrupted your practice. What can you learn from these experiences?

Ideal Clients		Non-ideal Clients

Craft your ideal client profile: Using the insights from the previous exercise, create a detailed profile of your perfect client. Consider demographics, psychographics, and behavioral traits. How will this profile guide your marketing and patient communication strategies?

My ideal client is: _____

_____

_____

_____

_____

_____

_____

_____

Align your practice with your ideal client: Review your current practice setup—your services, your marketing materials, and your intake process. How well do they align with the perfect client profile you've created? What changes can you make to attract better and serve your ideal clients?

Your brochures:

1._____

2._____

3._____

Your Website:

1._____

2._____

3._____

Facebook Ads:

1._____

2._____

3._____

Other marketing materials:

1. _____

2._____

3._____

Do they show pictures of your ideal clients? Do they appear to attract the person you are looking for? What words are you choosing? Or not choosing?

List some changes you need to make

This month

_____

_____

_____

_____

_____

_____

_____

_____

_____

_____

(3 month goal) This Quarter

_____

_____

_____

_____

_____

_____

_____

_____

_____

_____

_____

_____

_____

_____

(1 year goal) This year

_____

_____

_____

_____

_____

_____

_____

_____

_____

_____

_____

_____

_____

_____

Evaluate the messages you are sending into the world through this lens and see what improvements you can make to improve your connections to the ideal client. Show these changes to people in your practice who are already your ideal client and ask for their feedback. They can really help steer you in ways you were not expecting.

PUTTING PROCESSES INTO PLACE

In Chapter 5, *Putting Processes into Place,* I stress the essential role that well-defined systems and processes play in creating a successful, patient-centered healthcare practice. Processes are crucial—they ensure consistency, operational efficiency, and the kind of high-quality experience that patients come to depend on. One of my key messages in this Chapter is to make decisions based on core values, not fear. When we base choices on our mission and purpose, we avoid pitfalls like inefficiencies, patient dissatisfaction, and financial instability.

I outline several critical areas for process development, each contributing significantly to practice stability and growth:

1. **Financial Model**: Choosing an economic model—whether cash-based or insurance-dependent—is foundational, as it shapes everything from pricing to patient interactions and administrative responsibilities.
2. **Patient Scheduling and Onboarding**: A streamlined approach to scheduling and onboarding allows us to offer accessibility and set clear expectations with new patients. With suitable materials, onboarding

becomes a practical introduction to the practice, covering services, patient expectations, and necessary paperwork.

3. **Marketing and Testimonials**: Collecting patient testimonials (written or video) is invaluable, as they build credibility and help attract new patients.

4. **Payment Collection**: Effective payment collection systems, including online payment options, are essential for smooth revenue flow, whether the practice is cash-only or insurance-based.

5. **Patient Communication**: Consistent updates through email, texts, or portals keep patients engaged and improve satisfaction by making it easy for them to stay connected to their care.

I also emphasize the importance of innovation in practice management. Offering conveniences like online booking, telemedicine, and extended hours helps meet the needs of today's busy patients. Embracing technology—such as EHRs and patient portals—makes our practice more efficient and engages patients by giving them easy access to their health information. The team's consistent application of these processes is vital, as it not only ensures that the practice runs smoothly but also helps patients adhere to policies and protocols.

In "Dr. Michael Evan's Journey," I illustrate how implementing clear procedures transformed his practice flow and patient adherence. By pausing to put systems in place, he found that patients were more consistent with their appointments, and he could focus on higher-level tasks rather than day-to-day operations. These processes laid a solid foundation for his practice to grow while also creating a rewarding experience for his patients.

Please refer to page 75 in Chapter 5 for more details.

- **Process mapping**: Choose one key area of your practice (such as patient onboarding, payment collection, and appointment scheduling) and create a detailed process map. List each step, assign responsibilities, and note the required tools or resources. What steps do you need to take first? Who will you need to hire or consult to ensure your practice is set up correctly? What gaps or inefficiencies do you notice, and how can you address them?

_____

_____

_____

_____

_____

_____

_____

- **Decision-making worksheet**: Take some time to write out the pros and cons of both cash-based and insurance-based models as they apply to your specific situation. Consider factors such as patient population, financial goals, and your values as a healthcare provider. Research and analyze case studies of practices that have successfully implemented both models. What lessons can you learn from their experiences? How might these lessons inform your own decision?

Jason Sonners

_____

_____

_____

_____

_____

_____

- **Consultation with experts**: Schedule consultations with a business coach and a healthcare financial advisor to discuss your options. How can their insights help you clarify your decision and guide your next steps?

_____

_____

_____

_____

_____

_____

- **Vision board revisited**: Go back to your vision board, which represents the type of practice you want to build and update with the decisions you've made after this Chapter. Include images and words that reflect your choices (whether cash-based or insurance-based)

PUTTING PROCESSES INTO PLACE

and how they aligns with your overall goals for patient care and business success.

_____

_____

_____

_____

_____

_____

_____

- **Patient onboarding checklist**: Create a checklist for onboarding new patients. What information do they need? How will you ensure they feel welcome and informed? Consider the inclusion of educational materials, an introduction to your practice's policies, and a clear explanation of their treatment plan.

_____

_____

_____

_____

_____

_____

_____

- **Referral program design**: Design a referral program that incentivizes your current patients to refer others to your practice. What rewards will you offer? How will you promote the program? How will you track and manage referrals?

_____

_____

_____

_____

_____

_____

_____

After completing these exercises, you'll gain valuable insights into how to streamline your practice, enhance patient satisfaction, and attract new clients. These steps will help ensure your practice not only runs smoothly but also grows sustainably over time. By reflecting deeply on these questions and taking the steps needed to implement your decision, you'll be well on your way to building a practice that not only aligns with your professional goals but also serves your patients in the best possible way.

MAKING YOUR PRACTICE STAND OUT

In Chapter 6, *Making Your Practice Stand Out*, I discuss the importance of distinguishing your healthcare practice in a competitive market by building a robust and authentic brand. Effective marketing isn't simply about selling services; it's about connecting deeply with potential patients by communicating our values, expertise, and commitment to exceptional care. As Simon Sinek says, "People don't buy what you do; they buy why you do it," and I encourage practitioners to focus on this principle. By promoting our "why" and showing patients that we genuinely care, we can establish trust and long-lasting relationships.

To start standing out, practitioners must actively engage with their communities and potential patients through various channels: social media, local events, and networking opportunities. Effective marketing means being visible and accessible. For example, highlighting our specialized services—like Hyperbaric Oxygen Therapy or red light therapy—gives our practice a unique appeal, mainly when these therapies may not be widely available in our area.

Jason Sonners

Creating a Compelling Brand

Building a distinct brand goes beyond a memorable logo or tagline; it encompasses every patient interaction, from the front desk to the website. A well-crafted brand identity should reflect our values and provide a consistent experience that reassures patients they're in the right place. When patients sense a cohesive, caring environment, they're more likely to trust our services and refer others.

Adding Convenience and Innovation

Offering conveniences such as online booking, telemedicine options, and extended hours is critical to making our practice more appealing, especially to busy patients. Leveraging technology—such as electronic health records (EHRs) and patient portals—can streamline operations and give patients easy access to their health information, fostering greater engagement and satisfaction.

Delivering Exceptional Patient Care

Ultimately, the most effective way to differentiate a practice is by delivering exceptional care. Beyond clinical expertise, creating a comfortable, attentive, and patient-centered experience fosters loyalty and encourages referrals. Patients who feel genuinely cared for become powerful advocates for our practice.

Case Study: Dr. Michael Evan's Journey

Dr. Michael Evans' journey in this Chapter illustrates the power of branding and patient engagement. By emphasizing his unique strengths—like integrating traditional and alternative therapies—and investing in his online presence, he was able to connect with patients who value holistic care. From a memorable website to a structured follow-up system, every aspect of his brand was designed to enhance trust and visibility. This approach helped him reach more patients and build a practice that resonated with his values.

Please refer to page 94 in Chapter 6 for more details.

- **Brand identity exercise**: Define your practice's unique value proposition. What makes your practice different from others? Develop a tagline and list the core values that you want your brand to communicate. How can you ensure that every aspect of your practice, from your logo to patient interactions, reflects your brand identity? Does your current brand reflect the direction you now see your practice going?

_____

_____

_____

_____

_____

_____

- **Patient experience audit**: Conduct a patient experience audit. Walk through your practice as if you were a new patient, from scheduling an appointment to follow-up care. Identify any areas where the experience could be improved and outline steps to address them.

Jason Sonners

_____

_____

_____

_____

_____

_____

- **Website evaluation**: If you already have a website, evaluate its effectiveness. Is it user-friendly? Does it accurately reflect your practice's values and services? Consider hiring a professional to audit your website and suggest improvements. If you don't have a website, outline the key features you need and plan how to get it built.

_____

_____

_____

_____

_____

_____

_____

- **SEO and content strategy**: Develop an SEO and content strategy for your practice. Identify three to five key topics relevant to your target audience and create a content calendar for blog posts, videos, or social media updates. How will you measure the success of your content strategy?

_____

_____

_____

_____

_____

_____

- **Marketing plan development**: Develop a basic marketing plan for your practice. What strategies will you use to attract new patients? Consider SEO, social media, online ads, and referral programs. Set specific goals and timelines for implementing these strategies.

_____

_____

_____

_____

_____

_____

- **Marketing plan refinement**: Choose three marketing strategies from the list provided in this Chapter and develop a detailed plan for implementing them over the next three months. Set specific goals for each strategy, such as increasing website traffic, generating more patient referrals, or enhancing your social media presence.

  _____

  _____

  _____

  _____

  _____

  _____

- **Referral program design**: Design or refine your patient referral program. What incentives will you offer? How will you promote the program to your existing patients? How will you track and measure the success of your referral efforts?

  _____

  _____

  _____

  _____

  _____

  _____

By completing these exercises, you'll gain a deeper understanding of how to make your practice stand out in a competitive market. These steps will help you create a strong brand, attract your ideal patients, and build a practice that thrives both in-person and online.

THE FOUR TYPES OF CLIENTS

In Chapter 7, *The Four Types of Clients,* I explore the significance of understanding personality types in effective patient communication. The core idea here is that communication isn't just about sharing information; it's about building trust and ensuring that patients feel genuinely heard and understood. Tony Robbins' insight, "We are all different in the way we perceive the world," encapsulates this well. Healthcare providers often experience smoother connections with some patients and challenges with others, which frequently comes down to differences in communication and personality types.

I introduce four primary personality types—director, Socializer, Relater, and Thinker—each with distinct ways of receiving and processing information. Recognizing these types can dramatically improve how we connect with patients and increase their adherence to care plans. This approach ensures that patients receive information in a way that resonates with them, enhancing patient satisfaction and compliance.

Here's a summary of the types:

1. **Director**: Goal-oriented and results-focused, Directors appreciate direct and efficient communication. They prefer practical information

and a clear, results-driven path to achieving their health goals.

2. **Socializer**: This type values personal connections and enjoys a positive, engaging experience. Socializers are more receptive to treatments presented in a dynamic and collaborative way and may be motivated by the social aspects of their health journey.

3. **Relater:** Relaters prioritize harmony and strong relationships with their providers. They are comforted by empathetic interactions, appreciate encouragement, and seek a healthcare experience that addresses emotional as well as physical health.

4. **Thinker**: Thinkers want detailed, logical information and tend to be analytical in their decision-making. They prefer evidence-based explanations and often do additional research to feel confident in their healthcare choices.

By tailoring communication to each type, we can transform patient interactions, making them more personalized and effective. This personalized approach not only improves compliance but also strengthens patient-provider relationships. Patients who feel understood are more likely to become loyal advocates, leading to valuable word-of-mouth referrals and a more robust practice reputation.

In the case study of "Dr. Michael Evan's Journey," Michael struggles with communicating effectively across different patient types until his mentor introduces him to the concept of personality typing. By adjusting his approach, Michael builds stronger patient connections, which improves compliance and overall patient outcomes, reinforcing the benefits of personalized communication strategies.

Please refer to page 120 in Chapter 7 for more details.

- **Personality typing exercise**: Reflect on your interactions with recent patients. Identify which of the four personality types (Director, Socializer, Relater, Thinker) each patient aligns with. How did your communication style match or differ from their preferred style? What adjustments could you make in the future to improve communication with each type?

_____

_____

_____

_____

_____

_____

- **Personality self-assessment**: Take this personality assessment yourself to better understand your communication style. Reflect on how your personality type might influence your interactions with patients and how you can adapt to meet their needs more effectively.

_____

_____

_____

_____

_____

_____

- **Do the same and workshop these concepts with your staff**: Learn how to communicate better with your team as well!

_____

_____

_____

_____

_____

- **Role-playing scenarios**: Pair up with a colleague or friend to practice communicating with each of the four personality types. Take turns role-playing as both the patient and the health care provider, focusing on adapting your communication style to fit each personality type. After each scenario, discuss what worked well and what could be improved.

_____

_____

_____

_____

_____

- **Patient communication plan**: Choose a challenging patient from your practice and develop a communication plan based on their personality type. Outline specific strategies you will use in your next interaction to build rapport and improve communication. Using the insights from this Chapter, write a detailed plan on how you can rebuild trust with this patient by adapting your communication style. Include specific actions you will take to ensure they feel valued and understood.

_____

_____

_____

_____

_____

_____

_____

_____

- **Communication reflection journal**: Keep a journal where you reflect on your daily interactions with patients. Note which communication strategies were successful and which could improve. Over time, use these reflections to refine your approach and become more adept at tailoring your communication to each patient's personality.

_____

_____

_____

_____

_____

_____

Review the open-ended questions provided in the Chapter. Select three patients from your current practice and use these questions in your next session to assess their personality types. Record their responses and identify which personality type they most closely align with.

For each of the three patients you assessed, write down how you would adapt your communication style to better connect with them based on their identified personality type. Include specific phrases, tone adjustments, and approaches you will use to ensure they feel understood and respected.

Completing these exercises will enhance your ability to communicate effectively with a diverse range of patients. This will not only improve patient satisfaction but also lead to better health outcomes and stronger, more trusting relationships within your practice.

NURTURING YOUR IDEAL CLIENT

In Chapter 8, *Nurturing Your Ideal Client,* I focus on building long-term relationships with patients as a foundation for a thriving practice. It's not enough to simply bring patients in for initial appointments; the key to sustainable growth lies in consistently showing patients that we genuinely care about their well-being. This Chapter highlights that patients who feel valued and supported are more likely to remain loyal to your practice, refer others, and contribute to a positive, supportive environment.

A strong patient relationship goes beyond treatment—it's about ongoing communication, support, and engagement. I encourage healthcare practitioners to consider whether they aim to keep patients throughout all phases of their health journey or focus solely on specific treatments. Both approaches shape the nature and identity of the practice. To nurture these relationships effectively, here are some key strategies:

1. **Empathy as a Trust Builder**: Establishing a genuine connection with patients through empathy creates trust and encourages long-term relationships. Patients need to feel that their provider cares not only about their immediate concerns but also about their broader health journey.

Jason Sonners

2. **Implementing a Patient Recall System**: A systematic approach to re-engage patients who have missed appointments or fallen off the schedule helps retain patients over time. Personalizing outreach, following up, and maintaining accurate contact information foster a sense of continuity and care.

3. **Consistency in Follow-Up**: Simple follow-ups, like a call after the first visit, show commitment to the patient's long-term well-being. Even after a treatment plan ends, occasional check-ins can reassure patients that they are valued beyond the immediate scope of their care.

4. **Word-of-Mouth Growth**: When patients feel genuinely cared for, they often become advocates for your practice, bringing in new patients. Investing in these relationships can lead to higher retention rates and organic growth as loyal patients refer friends and family.

In "Dr. Michael Evan's Journey," featured in this Chapter, Michael learns that cultivating a supportive, patient-focused environment is not just about appointments and treatment—it's about creating a practice that patients see as a trusted health resource. Through regular follow-ups and personalized outreach, Michael fosters relationships that encourage patients to return and refer others, strengthening his practice as a true community of care.

Please refer to page 139 in Chapter 8 for more details.

1. **Map the phases of care**: Identify where your current patients are

within the three phases of care (active, maintenance, wellness). Develop a tailored strategy for each patient that addresses their specific needs within their current phase. Recognize that you may offer a range of different services or therapies. Specific tools may be more important or more effective during various phases of care. Additionally, the frequency, duration, and or intensity of your services may vary depending on the phase a patient is in. Think this through and develop a plan for how to recommend and implement shifts in their strategy based on the phase they are in.

_____

_____

_____

_____

_____

_____

2. **Plan client check-ins**: Create a plan for regularly checking in with your clients. Decide on the frequency (one week after the appointment or monthly follow-ups) and the method of communication (phone calls, emails, text messages). Outline what you will say during these check-ins to ensure they are meaningful and supportive.

_____

_____

_____

_____

_____

_____

_____

_____

3. **Personalize follow-up templates**: Develop a set of templates for personalized follow-up communications. These could include email templates for checking in after an appointment, offering additional resources, or celebrating a client's progress. Customize these templates based on different client needs and situations.

_____

_____

_____

_____

_____

_____

4. **Empathy in action**: Reflect on a recent client interaction where empathy played a significant role. What did you do or say that made the client feel understood and supported? How can you apply this approach to other clients? Write down your thoughts and plan to

incorporate these empathetic practices into your daily interactions.

_____

_____

_____

_____

_____

_____

_____

5. **Build professional relationships**: Create a plan for building and maintaining relationships with other healthcare providers. List potential providers in your area, outline how you'll introduce yourself, and set goals for how many new relationships you want to establish over the next quarter.

_____

_____

_____

_____

_____

_____

_____

CRAFTING YOUR FINANCIAL PLAN

In Chapter 9, *Crafting Your Financial Plan,* I dive into the importance of establishing a solid financial foundation for your practice. Understanding and managing finances isn't just about generating profit—it's about ensuring your practice has the resources to provide top-notch care sustainably. Many practitioners are uncomfortable discussing finances, but as I highlighted, an effective practice must balance its mission with financial viability. Critical components of a financial plan include setting fees that align with the quality of care, tracking income and expenses, and making informed decisions to keep the practice financially healthy.

Some of the main points covered are:

1. **Setting Fees with Integrity**: It's essential to price services appropriately to reflect their value. Underpricing can lead to resentment or burnout while overpricing may alienate patients. I recommend researching industry rates and selecting a pricing level that feels a little uncomfortable but fair—often a sign that you're valuing your services correctly.

2. **Financial Metrics for Practice Health**: Tracking financial data,

such as patient visit averages and revenue per patient, helps gauge practice efficiency and identify areas for improvement. Regular analysis of these metrics provides insights that support informed decision-making.

3. **Revenue Goals and Budgeting**: Establishing clear revenue goals and a budget enables a sustainable cash flow that covers all operational costs and supports personal income. Budgeting also reveals opportunities for growth, helping practitioners allocate resources strategically.

4. **Long-Term Financial Planning**: Beyond immediate financial goals, it's crucial to plan for the future by saving, investing, and considering expenses like retirement or business expansion. Practitioners should also evaluate tax-efficient strategies, which can benefit both personal and business finances.

In "Dr. Michael Evan's Journey," I illustrate how Michael begins to understand his practice's financial metrics and uses them to adjust pricing and improve service offerings. Initially hesitant, he finds that focusing on financial metrics doesn't detract from patient care—instead, it strengthens his ability to provide it by making his practice financially robust.

Please refer to page 154 in Chapter 9 for more details.

o **Analyze your practice's financial health**: Start by gathering vital financial statistics for your practice, such as total new patients, total visits, patient visit averages (PVA), total revenue, case average (lifetime patient value), and office visit average (OVA). What do these numbers tell you about the financial health of your practice?

	Month	Annual Total	Next Year Goals
Gross Collections			
New Patients			
Total Visits			
Case			
OVA			
PVA			

Case average or Lifetime value = Total revenue / Total new patients

OVA = Total revenue / Total visits

PVA = Total visits / Total new patients

Jason Sonners

o **Set your fees**: Research what other practices in your area are charging. Consider your unique value proposition and set your fees at a level that reflects the quality of care you provide. How do you feel about the fees you've set? Do they align with your values and the level of service you offer? After a long day at work, calculate how much revenue you brought in that day. Does that number feel rewarding to you or disappointing? This can be an easy way to gauge the long-term likelihood of how sustainable your current fee structure is.

_____

_____

_____

_____

_____

o **Create a financial plan**: Using the insights from your economic analysis, create a financial plan for your practice. What are your revenue goals for the next year? What strategies will you use to achieve them? How will you ensure that your practice remains financially healthy while continuing to provide exceptional care?

_____

_____

_____

CRAFTING YOUR FINANCIAL MASTER PLAN PART TWO

In Chapter 10, *Crafting Your Financial Master Plan, Part Two,* I delve into the specifics of managing financial health at a more detailed level, focusing on accurately calculating and managing the cost of goods sold (COGS) and understanding gross profit margins. This Chapter emphasizes that financial knowledge is essential for making informed decisions that not only keep your practice sustainable but also allow it to grow. By understanding these costs, you can strategically price services, manage resources, and optimize profitability without sacrificing quality.

Essential points covered include:
1. **Calculating Cost of Goods Sold (COGS)**: In healthcare, COGS isn't always straightforward. For service-based practices, COGS includes payroll for staff directly providing the services and the costs of consumables like medical supplies or oxygen for hyperbaric treatments. Knowing your COGS enables you to assess the true

profitability of each service.

2. **Gross Profit Margin:** Once COGS is calculated, determining gross profit margins becomes easier. This metric (gross profit divided by total revenue) gives a snapshot of financial health, helping you make data-driven decisions about pricing, staffing, and service offerings.

   Gross profit = Total revenue − COGS

   Gross profit margin = Gross profit / total revenue.

3. **Tracking Key Financial Metrics**: Monitoring metrics like revenue per room, occupancy rate, and gross profit per patient reveals inefficiencies and growth opportunities. These insights allow you to make adjustments, such as optimizing room usage, which may lead to offering additional services or revisiting pricing structures.

4. **Strategic Financial Planning**: I discuss options for reducing tax burdens and increasing savings, including tax-efficient investment strategies, retirement accounts, and health savings accounts. Establishing a tax-efficient structure for the business and engaging in long-term financial planning is crucial to maintaining both personal and professional financial healthvan's Journey," Michael realizes the power of understanding financial metrics. As he becomes more comfortable with concepts like COGS and occupancy rates, he begins to see his practice through a new lens, using these insights to make strategic decisions that support sustainable growth. By actively managing his financial data, he positions his practice for long-term success while continuing to provide exceptional patient care.

Please refer to page 168 in Chapter 10 for more details.

o **Calculate your COGS**: Start by identifying the direct costs associated with delivering your services. This includes payroll for staff directly involved in patient care and any consumable items used in treatments. Calculate your COGS for a specific service or your entire practice. How does this compare to your total revenue? What does this tell you about the profitability of your services?

o List the COG and its associated cost:

_____

_____

_____

_____

o **Determine your gross profit margin**: Using the COGS you calculated, determine your gross profit margin by dividing your gross profit by your total revenue. What is your current gross profit margin? Are there areas where you can improve it by either increasing revenue or reducing costs?

_____

_____

_____

_____

o **Total revenue and subtract total COGS:**

_____

_____

_____

_____

_____

_____

o **Track critical metrics**: Begin tracking essential metrics for your practice, such as revenue per room, clinic occupancy rate, and lifetime gross profit per patient. What do these metrics reveal about how efficiently your practice is utilizing its resources? Based on these insights, are there opportunities to increase revenue or reduce costs?

_____

_____

_____

_____

_____

_____

_____

o **Create an Action Plan to Improve Your Practice's Economic Health:** This could include strategies to increase patient volume and optimize room usage, reduce costs, or adjust pricing. Set specific goals and timelines for implementing these changes.

_____

_____

_____

_____

_____

_____

For example, let's consider the impact of marketing efforts on new patient acquisition. Suppose a clinic typically sees eight new patients per month but implements a successful marketing campaign, resulting in twelve new patients per month instead. In that case, the increase of four new patients per month multiplied by the average case value (for example, $3,053) yields a substantial monthly revenue increase of over $12,000.

Similarly, initiatives aimed at extending patient engagement and increasing PVA can significantly impact revenue generation. Suppose a clinic's PVA increases from twenty-two to thirty through educational efforts or monthly health challenges, resulting in an additional eight visits per month per patient. In this scenario, a clinic with four hundred monthly visits could potentially increase to 450 visits per month without the need for additional new patients.

The financial implications of this increased patient engagement are considerable. With eight more visits per person per month, multiplied by the average revenue per visit (like $137), the clinic stands to generate an additional $1,000 per person per month in income.

By manipulating these metrics and analyzing various scenarios, healthcare providers can gauge the potential impact of different strategies on the business's financial health. This data-driven approach empowers providers to identify opportunities for growth, optimize resource allocation, and drive sustainable business success in a competitive healthcare landscape.

CHAPTER 11

FINAL REVIEW

Please refer to page 176 in Chapter 11 for more details.

Final reflection: Reflect on your journey through this book and your *Field Guide For The Fulfilled Physician*. What are the most significant lessons you've learned? How have you grown as a practitioner and as a person? Write down your thoughts and any remaining questions or challenges you want to address.

o **Setting future goals**: Based on what you've learned, set three specific, measurable, and actionable goals for your practice over the next year. Outline the steps you need to take to achieve these goals and consider potential challenges and how you'll overcome them.

o **Building your legacy**: Consider the legacy you want to leave through your practice. What impact do you want to have on your patients, your community, and the field of health care? Write a statement of purpose that reflects your long-term vision and the values you want to uphold.

o **Creating your support network**: Identify critical individuals

Jason Sonners

and resources that will support you as you continue to grow your practice. This could include mentors, professional networks, educational resources, or team members. Develop a plan to engage with and strengthen this support network.

CLOSING THOUGHTS

Final Reflections: Your Path to Lasting Fulfillment

As you've reached the final pages of this field guide, pause for a moment and reflect on the transformative journey you've embarked upon. This guide, meticulously crafted, has not simply provided you with tasks and exercises. It has offered a structured pathway toward creating the practice—and life—you've always envisioned. The intentionality woven into each chapter is designed not to accelerate you through to completion, but rather to slow you down, prompting deep reflection and genuine clarity at every step.

Building a truly fulfilling practice requires careful integration of two essential pillars: emotional and financial success. While many healthcare professionals achieve mastery in clinical skills, few attain the harmony of inner fulfillment coupled with financial prosperity. This harmony is critical—not just for your own longevity and happiness but also for the quality of care you deliver to your patients and the atmosphere you create for your team.

Why Financial and Emotional Success Must Coexist

Financial success alone often leaves practitioners feeling empty, disconnected from their initial motivations, and burned out from chasing numbers rather than purpose. On the other hand, emotional fulfillment without financial viability leads to stress, scarcity, and diminished capacity to serve others effectively. Your fulfillment lies precisely in the intersection of these two worlds, each reinforcing and amplifying the other.

This field guide has prompted you to rigorously define what success means for you in both financial and emotional dimensions. Perhaps for you, emotional success means having deep, meaningful connections with your patients and seeing transformative changes in their health. Financial success might be reflected in achieving stability, having the freedom to invest in your practice, pursue innovation, reward your staff, and live the lifestyle you've envisioned. However you've defined these terms, the key is clarity and intentionality.

Each Step Matters Deeply

Throughout the exercises provided, you've confronted foundational questions and made critical decisions about your core values, ideal patient profiles, financial strategies, and communication styles. Each reflection was designed not simply to be completed, but to encourage meaningful contemplation and authentic insight. It's crucial to remember: **this journey is not a race.** It's a purposeful, mindful progression towards the practice and life you desire.

The depth of time and honest introspection you invest in each exercise directly correlates to the authenticity and resilience of the practice you build. Rushing through tasks merely to "finish" undermines the very transformation this guide aims to facilitate. True growth, both professionally and personally, happens when you deliberately slow down and engage deeply with each concept, challenging yourself to look beyond the surface.

Jason Sonners

The Big Picture: Crafting Your Vision

At the heart of this guide is the understanding that success in practice comes from careful planning and precise alignment with your core purpose. Every chapter, from clarifying your identity and purpose to defining processes and nurturing relationships plays a pivotal role in constructing a stable, thriving, and joyful practice.

By clearly articulating your vision and aligning it with concrete actions, you set the stage for consistent, fulfilling, and prosperous days ahead. Your clarity regarding who you want to be, how you want to practice, and whom you wish to serve informs all strategic decisions. This vision acts as a compass, helping you make choices in alignment with your ultimate goals and purpose.

Designing with Intention

A significant strength of the exercises you've completed is their collective emphasis on intentionality. From your practice's layout and patient experience to your team culture and marketing approach, each element is designed with purpose. This intentionality not only differentiates your practice from others but ensures it authentically represents your values and mission. Patients feel the difference, your staff thrives in the clarity, and you enjoy a greater sense of control and satisfaction in your work.

Mastering Relationships and Communication

Integral to your fulfillment is the depth and authenticity of your relationships. By understanding and applying the different communication styles introduced, you've learned to meet patients where they are, communicate effectively, and deepen trust. Your intentional communication fosters patient adherence, improves outcomes, and naturally generates enthusiastic

Jason Sonners

referrals, further reinforcing both emotional and financial success.

Financial Clarity and Mastery

This guide emphasized that financial clarity is not just essential for business viability—it's crucial for personal peace of mind. By examining your pricing, defining your service offerings, and understanding your core financial metrics, you've established a financial foundation that is both robust and adaptable. Such clarity empowers you to make informed decisions, manage resources effectively, and ensure your practice remains sustainable and prosperous.

Understanding concepts like cost of goods sold (COGS) and gross profit margins isn't merely academic—it's empowering. These insights let you confidently adjust your approach, innovate your offerings, and strategically expand your practice without compromising your values or patient care quality.

Integration: Your Fulfillment Blueprint

Ultimately, the power of this guide lies in integration—each exercise and insight forming an interconnected blueprint for your ideal practice. Every decision about identity, every exercise on patient relationships, and every financial calculation is a brick in the foundation of a practice that truly fulfills you.

This integration is more than strategic—it's emotional. You build not just a healthcare practice, but a vibrant community. You foster relationships based on authenticity, empathy, and mutual respect. Your financial decisions ensure sustainability, giving you the freedom to continue doing what you love, and to do it exceptionally well.

Jason Sonners

Commitment to Ongoing Growth

Fulfillment is not a static destination but an ongoing journey. Regularly revisit these exercises, update your vision board, re-assess your core values, and recalibrate your financial strategies as your practice evolves. This ongoing commitment to reflection and adaptation ensures continued growth, satisfaction, and prosperity.

Your practice is a living entity—it grows, shifts, and evolves. You, too, evolve with it. Staying flexible, curious, and committed to ongoing reflection allows you to continuously align your actions with your evolving vision of success.

Building Your Legacy

As you look ahead, consider your legacy—what lasting impact you wish to have on your patients, community, and the field of healthcare. Your deliberate planning today defines that legacy tomorrow. Every patient interaction, staff training, and strategic decision contributes to your lasting imprint. Keep your purpose and legacy clearly visible, as they anchor your daily actions and long-term vision.

Your Next Steps

This is your moment of commitment. The Field Guide has equipped you with clarity, purpose, and actionable strategies. Now, take deliberate, confident steps toward your envisioned practice. Implement thoughtfully, reflect continuously, and adjust proactively.

Remember, fulfillment is about alignment—the alignment of who you are, how you practice, the relationships you cultivate, and the financial choices you make. Honor each component with care and attention. Embrace the slower pace required for thoughtful growth and celebrate each incremental achievement.

You've invested deeply in this journey, and your practice is poised to reflect your authentic values and passions. Let this Field Guide be your ongoing companion, offering clarity and structure whenever you feel uncertain or inspired to recalibrate. Your ideal practice—the one that meets both your emotional needs and financial goals—is within reach. With intentionality, patience, and continuous reflection, it's not just possible, it's inevitable.

Congratulations on choosing the path of true fulfillment. The future you've envisioned is ready and waiting for you. Go confidently forward.

Order Your Copy Today

The Fulfilled Physician
Your Dream Practice Blueprint

Jason Sonners

ABOUT THE AUTHOR

Dr. Jason Sonners is a distinguished chiropractor and PhD in molecular biology with expertise in regenerative medicine with a passion for helping people achieve optimal health and well-being. With a deep understanding of integrative therapies, Dr. Sonners blends chiropractic care with cutting-edge treatments like HBOT, IV therapies, light therapies, and nutrition to support healing, improve performance, and enhance overall health. He has dedicated his career to advancing holistic health solutions, advocating for the use of natural therapies to treat chronic conditions, enhance recovery, and promote longevity.

Driven by a desire to make a broader impact, Dr. Sonners has devoted himself to research, education, and expanding the accessibility of HBOT to healthcare professionals and patients alike. He is an active speaker and author, sharing his knowledge with practitioners worldwide, empowering them to integrate additional healing modalities and functional medicine strategies into their practices. Dr. Sonners is also a faculty and board member of both the International Board of Undersea Medicine and the International Hyperbaric

Jason Sonners

Association, a testament to his commitment to excellence in this specialized field.

In addition to his clinical work, Dr. Sonners is the owner and director of HBOT USA, where he mentors practitioners, equipping them with the knowledge and tools needed to successfully implement HBOT in their practices. His mission is not only to offer exceptional care to his own patients but also to ensure that more people can benefit from the profound healing effects of oxygen therapy by making it more accessible.

Beyond his clinical and educational pursuits, Dr. Sonners's passion for expanding access to proper treatments and high-quality care has led him to consult with clinics and health care providers around the world. By helping businesses grow, streamline operations, and implement HBOT, light therapies, IV nutrition and other therapies, he supports practitioners in creating thriving practices that achieve both clinical excellence and business success. Dr. Sonners's ultimate goal is to bridge the gap between cutting-edge health solutions and the patients who need them most.

Connect With The Author

Jason Sonners

HBOT USA - YouTube

(8) Jason Sonners | LinkedIn

support@hbotusa.com

Home - Hyperbaric Oxygen NJ (hbotusa.com)

www.ingramcontent.com/pod-product-compliance
Lightning Source LLC
Chambersburg PA
CBHW082108210326
41599CB00033B/6638